DUCKI

TOM CROMHOUT

ISBN 978-0-620-52757-6
Published by Reach Publishers, P O Box 1384, Wandsbeck, South Africa, 3631
Printed and bound by Mega Digital

Edited by Susan Van Tonder for Reach Publishers
Cover designed by Reach Publishers

Website: www.aimtoinspire.com
E-mail - reach@webstorm.co.za

Dedication

To my team of 2002 to 2005, who inspired me by making me think and ask myself what the reasons were for the underperformance of our team.

What a life-changing experience, with the birth of

DUCKI!

Contents

Chapter 1

Eleven o'clock on the evening of the 15ᵗʰ July 2002!

It was our month end and I was driving home after missing our target by a very small margin, which to me is totally unacceptable as I am a winner by nature and have a record and reputation of not missing targets.

I had just been promoted to General Manager Operations in the blue chip chain of the largest and most successful furniture retail company in South Africa.

Driving home feeling very disappointed that we had

not achieved all our targets (goals) for the month as a team, I asked myself: what is the problem that we get so close, but not quite there? I started playing with words, asking myself: Is it that the Discipline of the team is not in place? Are the Urgency levels of every team member what they should be? I thought on, wondering if all the people had the necessary Knowledge – were they all trained and equipped? Did they always know what was expected from them and how to go about achieving it?

It was also clear to me that every member of the team was not fully Committed as a team player to achieving the team's targets. Finally, I realised that there is not enough Involvement from every individual, including the team leaders or management.

I started saying to myself: "<u>D</u>iscipline, <u>U</u>rgency, <u>C</u>ommitment, <u>K</u>nowledge, <u>I</u>nvolvement" over and over. To remember the five words I said only the first letter of each word and realised that they spelled "DUCKI".

I thank God for giving DUCKI to me, as it is clear to me that only God could have made it so easy.

Arriving home I was so excited and could not wait to tell my wife, Debbie.

"I know now why my team didn't make it," I almost shouted,

"They have no DUCKI!!!"

"No DUCKI?" she asked, surprised and still a little sleepy.

I then explained to her that "DUCKI" stands for the Discipline, Urgency, Commitment, Knowledge and Involvement needed to achieve!

I was so excited, I could not wait for the next day to share DUCKI with my team, and get every member of the team to understand and buy into the importance of DUCKI in our lives and the daily doing of our jobs. I realised that,

"With DUCKI in line, everything MUST be fine."

Eleven o'clock on the evening of the 15th July 2002!

It so happened that I had asked the regional managers to inform their business unit managers who had not achieved their targets for the month to report to our boardroom the next day at nine o'clock for a motivational session.

Present at the motivational session were 15 of the 25 business unit managers, five regional managers and my divisional sales manager.

On the white board before everyone arrived for the session I had written in bold letters:

D-ISCIPLINE   **?!**

U-RGENCY   **?!**

C-OMMITMENT   **?!**

K-NOWLEDGE   **?!**

I-NVOLVEMENT   **?!**

After greeting everybody and thanking them for being present, I said to them, "Champs [the way I refer to my team members], I know what is missing or wrong with our team that we don't all always get there.

Everybody's

DUCKI

Is

Not

In

Line?!"

I got different reactions and looks from the team and then I started explaining to them the meaning of DUCKI by working through each word, asking:

DISCIPLINE

Are we sure that all the disciplines are in place in every one of our business units, every department and every individual and that they are working for everybody every day?

By "disciplines" I mean things like: starting on time and doing everything that should be done when it should be done.

I asked the managers, do they always lead by example?

URGENCY

Does everybody realise the urgency or importance of doing today's work today and of achieving daily targets every day?

COMMITMENT

Is every member of the team committed and do they all really feel they are part of the team?

Do they look at the big picture and realise how important each one of their individual performances is to the overall performance of the team?

Or do they believe that things are OK as long as they have made it?

Are they committed to what they have to do or say they will do?

KNOWLEDGE

Are we sure that each and every member of our teams has the knowledge to perform or do the job 100%, and do they always know what is expected from them and what the team wants or has to achieve?

INVOLVEMENT

This is a given for the person or people engaged in any activity, but for all of us, as managers, are we involved to make sure that the D, U, C, K and I of DUCKI are in place and that we do obtain the desired results from each individual and as a team?

Imagine you and your partner having sex with you in the lounge and your partner in the bedroom.

I HAD THE ATTENTION OF EVERYONE PRESENT AND THERE WAS A NOTICEABLE VIBE OF EXCITEMENT IN THE AIR.

WE THEN DISCUSSED MANAGING ALL THE MANAGERS' TEAMS DAILY WITH EVERYONE'S DUCKI IN LINE.

Chapter 2

Care, but really care

Being a furniture retail company selling on credit to the public, our daily activities include:

- selling
- delivering and
- collecting the cash

DUCKI

Our work also involves:

- customer care
- caring for our staff
- administration and
- stock and cash control.

The most important of these activities is:

CUSTOMER CARE
AND
CARING FOR OUR STAFF.

It is vital in any business that we really care for our customers not only in what we say, but in the way we treat the customers from the first contact and for the rest of the relationship or for the customer's life for that matter.

First we must make the sales or we will have no cash to collect and in both the Sales and Credit departments, the most important focus is the customer and our most important activity is customer care.

For us as managers it is just as important that we really care for our staff, by getting to know every individual and finding out the things that are important to them as a person and not only as an employee:

TRAINING, LEADING AND GUIDING THEM TO DEVELOP IN EVERY AREA OF THEIR LIVES.

Chapter 3

Applying DUCKI in sales

Q uestion:
Are all our DUCKIs in line when it comes to the way we treat our customers?

SALES

In the Sales Department we can apply DUCKI in these ways:

- Discipline – being friendly, attentive, helpful, courteous, probing, establishing need, prospecting, etc.;

- Urgency – realising the customer may have other things to do (might be in a hurry) when we're processing the sale and making sure that the delivery of the goods happens as promised, on time and in good condition;

- Commitment – always delivering what we commit to or promise so easily, and being committed to making sure that every customer is a satisfied and happy one;

- Knowledge – making sure that our product knowledge is up to standard and that every sales person has the knowledge to make the sale and do the administration that goes with it;

- Involvement – as managers being involved in training, coaching and closing sales.

Chapter 4

Applying DUCKI in collecting the cash

Q uestion:

Do we treat every customer with the same respect at all times whether it's one of our best existing customers, a new customer or a customer with problems who has become a bad debt?

COLLECTING THE CASH (CREDIT CONTROL):

I believe that every customer is a good customer and we create bad debts through poor or incorrect customer care.

In collecting the cash we can apply DUCKI in the following ways:

- **Discipline** – we should begin by explaining the contract to the customer and making sure that they know how much must be paid per month and when the first instalment is due; we need to tell the customer to report to the shop if anything happens that makes them unable to pay or if they have a problem with the goods.

- **Urgency** – we should explain why it is important to pay every month and why it is important for the customer to report to the shop if they have any problems with paying or with the goods.

- **Commitment** – we should attend to and assist every customer with financial difficulty or who has a problem with the goods by showing we care and without embarrassing the customer.

- **Knowledge** – we should obtain the knowledge we need through formal training and/or coaching by management. Knowing your customers and their circumstances is important. This can be done by interviewing the customers with problems to find out what the problem is. Did he lose his job or was there a death in the family etc.

- **Involvement** – management should train, coach, guide and assist staff with any problems.

The team left the meeting highly motivated and ready and excited to get back to their branches and get all their and their teams' DUCKIs in line.

Chapter 5

DUCKI or Ducking

I asked Jean, my secretary, to find us a nice picture of a cute DUCKI that we could use on all future daily and other memos to the branches. She found the picture that afternoon.

PICTURE OF DUCKI

We printed a copy of the DUCKI for each manager and staff member, explaining what DUCKI meant.

In the following few days I went out visiting my branches to make sure that every Champ knew what DUCKI meant. I told them that if anything was not going the way it should be, they would surely find the reason was that their DUCKI was not OK and this meant they were ducking!

The staff all enjoyed DUCKI and they all bought into DUCKI immediately, which resulted in a major improvement in all areas of the business in every department.

We exceeded all our targets every month for the next 12 consecutive months and are currently the most profitable division in the company, with a year-on-year growth in nett profit of 223.1%! In some cases individual performance improved by as much as 80%!

The same performance and growth continued for three years in a row until I left the company.

I received the award for Top Divisional General Manager Operations for three years and in every quarter over that time and so did many members of my team. Many staff in my team received promotions because of their personal growth.

We were a happy and successful team that earned a lot of money in performance bonuses while making a lot more money for the company.

Chapter 6

Keeping DUCKI alive

Starting from the birth of DUCKI on the 16th of July 2002, I sent a daily motivational sms to my divisional team and my secretary, who wrote it as a memo to all the branches, which was my way of keeping my DUCKIs in line and also of keeping DUCKI alive and top of mind for every staff member.

DUCKI

All employees were required to read the memo and sign that they acknowledged reading it.

This meant that every new staff member that started in our team was introduced to DUCKI on the first day as and when they read and signed the DUCKI memo.

Daily DUCKI figures were sent to every branch every morning to inform branch managers and staff of how they were doing month to date in comparison to all the other branches in our division.

The divisional team members got daily figures to show them how they and the division were doing compared to the rest of the company in every department.

The branch employees named these figures the DUCKI figures, and boy were they quick to phone if the figures were late.

When things were going a little slowly for a day or two, I immediately reminded all staff that there was a problem, that their DUCKIs are not in line.

From this comes the title of my book:

WITH DUCKIs IN LINE, ALL MUST BE FINE!

DUCKI

I went out looking for DUCKI in the form of a toy or an ornament and found our DUCKI sitting on an egg, which I painted gold.

How appropriate!

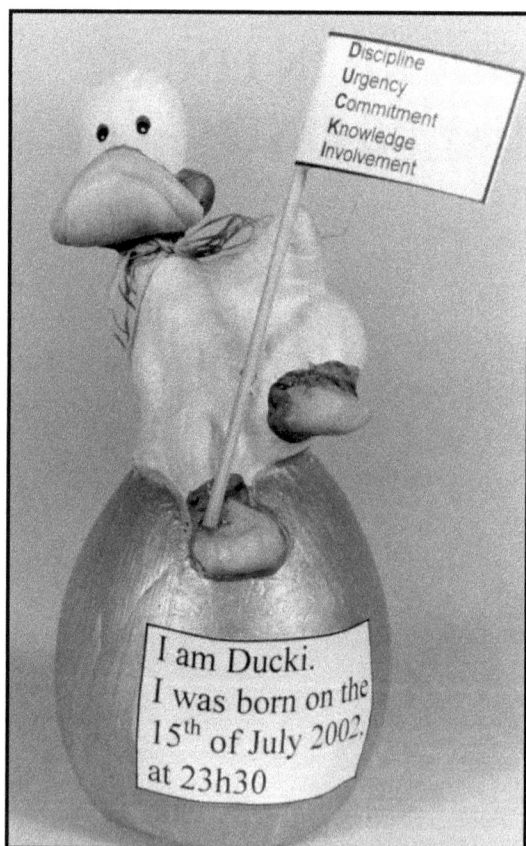

I bought every DUCKI in the shop and the owner of the shop told me that they couldn't get the same DUCKI again, which was wonderful for me to hear, knowing that no one but my team and I would have a DUCKI like our DUCKI.

I made a little flag explaining the meaning of DUCKI for every divisional team member.

I then went around every branch and presented DUCKI sitting on the golden egg holding the flag to every branch manager and staff member.

I also made a label that I stuck on the eggs that read:

"All the good things that life has to offer, waiting to hatch!"

Finally I had an 800 x 800 cm banner made that we took with us to our divisional meetings and chain meetings. We were really rubbing it in that we were the BEST!

The team was totally hooked on DUCKI; at every meeting someone would present me with some interesting duck that they bought for me: some were battery-operated, some puppets and there was a wide variety of ducks. Where had they found them?

Well I didn't ask.

We had DUCKI photographed by a professional photographer and had A4 posters made, which also feature on the front cover of this book.

Staff members wrote songs about DUCKI, which they and their teams would sing at our meetings. They had trophies made for monthly awards, and it was just going better and better every month!

One of the branch managers who did glass artwork as a hobby presented me with a stunning trophy he had made for me.

The story of DUCKI was truly a success story in the workplace and I couldn't have been more thrilled with the positive results and enthusiasm it generated. However, I then began to ponder, if it worked so well in the workplace, surely it could also be successfully applied to all other areas of our lives?

Chapter 7

DUCKI in all areas of our lives

When I began to think about it, I realised that "DUCKI" can have many other meanings which can help us in every area of our lives. It can stand for:

D - edication
U - nderstanding
C - ommunication
K - indness
I - nteraction

Or

D - evelop
U - nselfish
C - are
K - eel (to chill)
I - mprovement

The variations are endless.

Why not find your own?

Let's look at each one of the original five components of DUCKI in detail and how they apply to our lives.

DISCIPLINE

Having discipline involves things like being on time and not overindulging in anything. It also involves making time to develop every aspect of our lives – both private and professional – which includes our spiritual, intellectual, mental and physical wellbeing. It means that we must make time daily for (or to plan for) exercising, reading, studying, spiritual activity, communication with staff and family, social activity, eating and sleeping.

If we were taught all the disciplines and made them habits from the day we were born or from a very young age, we would go through life having fun, achieving and enjoying every aspect and day of our lives.

Discipline is doing what you must do when you must do it, and not doing what you should not be doing!

URGENCY

Having a sense of urgency involves things like meeting deadlines and doing things by when they must be done, knowing why we should do them by then. As such urgency is the twin of discipline. Urgency must not be confused with being urgent, like a ringing phone that is urgent and irritating. Something we treat with urgency is important, not urgent. Treating too many things as urgent is tiring and will lead to burn out. If we plan, as I mentioned under "Discipline", we will have very little that is urgent in our lives. We must work on our urgency level daily to achieve everything we want to or have to, when we want to or have to. It is knowing why and by when it must be done and doing it by then or before then that constitutes a positive sense of urgency.

COMMITMENT

Commitment is the desire to do or achieve something and can only be achieved if we know what we want to achieve, by when we want to or have to achieve it, and how to go about achieving it.

It is therefore important to make sure that we are clear on the "how", "what" and "by when" for us to be able to be committed to anything or to have commitment to it.

KNOWLEDGE

Knowledge involves knowing *what* is expected, *how* to do it, by *when* it must be done, by *whom* it must be done and *why* it must be done. Without the knowledge of any of the five, nothing will ever get done as and by when it must be done!

A very successful person I've known since he was a salesman and who is now in politics when asked if he was just lucky answered "yes" and wrote on a blackboard as follows:

LABOUR
UNDER
CONTROLLED
KNOWLEDGE

INVOLVEMENT

Without involvement, nothing can or will happen. That's right – someone or something is involved in every- and anything that takes place or that we want done. Take breathing – which we take for granted – it involves the person or living thing and oxygen! Any result we want to achieve, whether by man or machine, requires our involvement!

Now let's turn to how DUCKI applies to three important areas of our lives: our relationships with others, our weight, and our intellect or understanding.

DUCKI IN OUR RELATIONSHIPS WITH OTHERS:

- Discipline – involves things like being on time for an appointment, not overdoing things (e.g. drinking, disagreeing), and finding out the other person's likes and dislikes by listening to them.

- Urgency – involves first understanding the other person's urgency level or the importance to them of certain things or issues and then explaining to or telling the other person how you view these things and why.

- Commitment – there must be a commitment to or care from both parties for a relationship to succeed.

- Knowledge –we must not only know the other person, but we must also know their expectations, likes and dislikes or preferences to have a good relationship.

- Involvement – we must do things together that we both enjoy. Communication is and always will be the single most important way to be involved in any relationship. It is the start and the end of every relationship.

  Imagine having sex without being involved.

DUCKI AND YOUR WEIGHT:

- Discipline – involves never overindulging or eating and drinking food or beverages that cause weight gains and doing regular exercise, with the discipline to make or find the time for it.

- Urgency – involves realising the importance of having three or more smaller meals per day rather than having only one big unhealthy meal per day that causes you to overindulge and go to bed on a full stomach and having most of it stored as fat because you don't burn it.

- Commitment – involves committing yourself to a healthy eating lifestyle and exercise and to understanding why it is important.

- Knowledge – involves knowing and understanding your body and what is good or bad for you, as well as knowing what and when to eat or drink, and what and when not.

DUCKI AND OUR INTELLECT OR UNDERSTANDING:

- Discipline – involves listening to our families and staff or people we work with to make sure we understand what is important to them and what makes them tick.

- Urgency – involves understanding the importance of being attentive, and constantly improving our intellects.

- Commitment – is being committed to our staff and family's wellbeing because we care for them, making sure that we know them and we have the knowledge to lead them.

- Knowledge – it is important to know what is important and to make sure that we don't spend our time on things or activities that are of little or no benefit to us.

- Involvement – we show our involvement by spending time with our families and staff and by keeping ourselves busy with activities that will improve our understanding of them and of the things we have to have a good knowledge of.

Chapter 8

DUCKI starts with ME

Let's look at some other interesting DUCKI variations.

Delegate	Doers
Unto	Unity
Capable	Commonly
Knowledgeable	Knowing
Individuals	Importance

Drop	Doers
Until	Use
Commitment	Courage
Kept	Kindled
Inadvertently	Involvement
Develop	Deals
Until	Until
Commitment	Commitment
Knowledge	Kept
Inspired	Inadvertently

And there are many more that we can apply in our daily lives and activities.

DISCIPLINE

Discipline begins with self-discipline.

We cannot have a disciplined team or family if we don't start by leading from the front.

How can we discipline someone about something that we are also guilty of doing or not doing?

We can't – it begins with us, or me.

For example: If I am not always on time, how can I reprimand or be upset with someone else who is late?

URGENCY

If my urgency level is not what it should be and I do not always demonstrate that I know the importance of things, how can I expect the people around me to have the correct urgency levels?

COMMITMENT

To earn commitment from others in anything we must show our commitment through our knowledge and involvement. We must become doers and not only be talkers.

KNOWLEDGE

My knowledge in every area where I must lead must always be what it should be to enable me to lead with confidence and earn respect through my leadership. If I don't have the answer immediately, I must find it immediately without allowing people to doubt my capability. The same principle applies to management teams.

INVOLVEMENT

My involvement must always be present in everything I expect other people to perform: intense and regular in the beginning, becoming less intense and only periodical as my team becomes more committed through increased knowledge.

Chapter 9

DUCKI when we are studying

D UCKI when we are studying:

DISCIPLINE

When studying being disciplined starts on the first day of the first term and involves getting organised and making sure that I have everything I need to complete the final exam successfully, and being ready to do what must be done through proper and proactive planning.

URGENCY

Involves understanding the importance of doing and completing studying tasks and assignments daily and meeting all deadlines.

COMMITMENT

Comes when studying if and when we understand why we are studying our chosen subject and when we understand that we want to study to improve our intellect or to qualify ourselves better.

KNOWLEDGE

Doesn't always come from studying only; it is important as students for us to know and understand why it is important to study our chosen subject.

INVOLVEMENT

Is a given for the person doing the studies, but it also involves other people like teachers, and things like books and tapes – it is important that the balance is correct.

Here are a few more variations of DUCKI:

Dedicated	Develop
Unselfish	Unison
Care	Communication
Kindness	Kindle
Interaction	Initiative

Chapter 10

DUCKI as a sportman

D UCKI as a sportsman:

DISCIPLINE

In sports the most important ingredient to achieve is discipline, without which we can stop before we even start. Without disciplined regular training at the correct intensity we will not achieve much and will basically just be wasting our time and efforts.

URGENCY

If I don't realise the importance of training regularly I will not achieve much in sports.

COMMITMENT

Committing myself to achieving, having a set goal and making time for regular training will ensure success.

KNOWLEDGE

Involves knowledge of our capabilities and the requirements to achieve the level we want to achieve; this knowledge will help us to stay committed to our sport.

INVOLVEMENT

Is not negotiable in sport.

Chapter 11

DUCKI and my finances

D UCKI and my finances:

DISCIPLINE

That will help you sleep at night is, most importantly, not to spend more than you get in or earn! Don't spend your hard-earned money before it's in the bank and before you've sat down with your partner and worked out your budget. Also don't spend any money before you've paid all your monthly commitments. Like my mother used to say, "It never balances like it balances on paper." Don't fall into the trap of eating out on payday or getting takeaways, only to find you're short when you start paying your bills. Have a savings plan no matter how little you can put aside every month; this will grow and will help you through those unexpected emergencies and maybe pay for your next holiday.

URGENCY

We must understand the importance of paying bills on or before the due date, as this will save interest and other additional fees. We must also realise the importance of not spending on unnecessary things before we've calculated our budget and budgeted for necessary things.

COMMITMENT

Is of utmost importance in managing our finances. To be committed we must understand why we have to manage our finances, whether business or personal. This includes personal finances like balancing monthly household budgets, saving for that holiday we always wanted, a child going to university and other things right up to retirement. If we don't understand why we are doing it or what we are doing it for, there won't be any commitment.

KNOWLEDGE

Of balancing income and expenses is very important and will avoid embarrassment (e.g. running into debt, repossession, no cash at month-end, no cash for emergencies) and over-spending. Knowing what university costs will be in ten years from now, or how much money we will need ten years from now to have a liveable income is very important so that we can plan

DUCKI

our savings and avoid any nasty surprises when the time comes and we need the money.

INVOLVEMENT

Of ourselves and other people like brokers is essential for the successful managing of our finances.

Chapter 12

DUCKI in the garden

D^{UCKI} in the garden:

DISCIPLINE

When gardening is as important as discipline for anything else. We must have the discipline to maintain our gardens daily by watering, weeding, fertilising, keeping the soil loose, and cutting back and pruning plants when necessary and at the right time of the year if we want to have the garden that we wish for and expect.

URGENCY

Or the importance of maintaining our gardens to make something of them must be understood for us to keep it up. For this reason it will be wise to invest in a gardening book or to visit your local library to read about the do's and don'ts of gardening.

COMMITMENT

To having a beautiful garden can and will only be achieved if your desire to have one is strong enough and you have knowledge or the assistance of someone who has knowledge about the do's and don'ts of gardening. Being committed to your garden means taking care of it on a regular basis.

KNOWLEDGE

About gardening can be gained by studying but the best way to learn about your garden is through trial and error. Things like when and how to prune, or what to plant where in the garden and when to plant it, how deep to plant it and how much and what fertiliser to use, how often to water and how much water to use, for example, can be read in books or obtained by asking the staff at your local nursery. But your true knowledge will only really develop as you garden and find out for yourself what works best for your garden: things like finding out and knowing where the full shade, semi-shade and sunny areas of your garden are.

INVOLVEMENT

For a beautiful garden is a must, as with anything else that we want to make a success of.

Chapter 13

Good Luck

So we can apply DUCKI to every area of our lives and make life very enjoyable and fun and successful for everyone.

Go for it! Start first with the area of your life where you would like to be successful and which you find enjoyable!

Good luck and have fun.

www.ingramcontent.com/pod-product-compliance
Lightning Source LLC
Chambersburg PA
CBHW071841020426
42331CB00007B/1803